A Mountain of Past Lives & Things I've Learned

A Mountain of Past Lives & Things I've Learned

Skyler Jaye

BLAZEVOX[BOOKS]
Buffalo, New York

A Mountain Of Past Lives & Things I've Learned
By Skyler Jaye

Published by BlazeVOX [books]

Printed in the United States of America

Interior design and typesetting by Geoffrey Gatza
Cover Art: Daniel Morris

First Edition
ISBN: 978-1-60964-313-3
Library of Congress Control Number: 2018939203

BlazeVOX [books]
131 Euclid Ave
Kenmore, NY 14217
Editor@blazevox.org

publisher of weird little books

BlazeVOX [books]

blazevox.org

21 20 19 18 17 16 15 14 13 12 01 02 03 04 05 06 07 08 09 10

BlazeVOX

Acknowledgements

Mountains of Past-Lives and Things I've Learned was originally published in The Ghost City Review and was reprinted in the My Next Heart: New Buffalo Poetry anthology (BlazeVOX books, 2017)

The first Time was originally published in Germ Magazine.

LGBARTWORK was originally published in the My Next Heart: New Buffalo Poetry anthology.

Table of Contents

For Ted,
Thank you for loving me in every life.

A Mountain of Past Lives & Things I've Learned

A Mountain of Past-Lives
& Things I've Learned

I'm always learning mountains from other people.
Things like:
How climbing into courage takes
the use of knives, sometimes.
How someone can dig up the cracked skulls of
past lives with their bare hands.
How the let go can be the hardest part for one person,
and somehow the easiest part for the other.

Some mountains I've learned
should have come with "falling rock" signs,
a way to warn bystanders of what's to come.
I would beg forgiveness if I thought I needed to,
bash my knees into learned solitude of a varied terrain.
Instead we'll blame it on the people who taught me hatred:

I.

A woman. Watched wicked hands drape black ribbons
around inexperienced wrists.
Her eyes burned into naive ribcages while
they were broken by bartering men.
The darkness ate her. She let it devour her daughter.
There were seven years of bad luck for every bottle
she broke with her teeth,
passed on the omen to her children.
Left them stranded in her cursed slurs
while their childhood rotted
beneath her addict touch.
She found homes in men paying rent
with a daughter's body.
She never apologized.

II.

A cavalier smile of a man with black ribbons for hands,
sawed the bones of a girl with dreams bigger than a home
she was buried in.
Her lips bled for every year she saw
his predatory eyes in other people.
He never flinched at the bile in her throat,
and she never stopped bleeding.
A home draped in lust. Built the bridge from innocence
to damaged with the friction between his thighs,
led straight to a door he walked out of.
The disappearance act of a man with
decomposing skin
left space
between answers I was too young to ask for.
I'll live cautious until an obituary is written.

III.

An artist with a blemished tongue.
Busted stenciled-out fist marks found
on the pale skin
of his lover.
Swallowed the world out of her.
Took the body of a broken thing.
Broke it harder.
Warning signs flashed above blue rimmed
glasses and beneath broken fingernails.
He was a heartbeat dripping sin.
I swear I still feel healed bruises throbbing
when I think of him.
A mixed medium of
objections and unapologetic wounds.

Some days the climb gives me the vertigo
of falling into too much.
The mountain grew on shattered livelihood
And I've been stumbling my way through since
before I knew what lessons were.
What it meant to resent.
I'm always tracing back defeated footsteps
knowing exactly where they'll take me,
always hoping they won't.

Methods of the Voiceless

Hallow fills mouths that breathe
burdens into existence.
There's acceleration to reach the enlightenment
of how to hate yourself into decomposition.
Sweet vanity leaves blue marks on our lips.
Someone else's skin rubs mine gone,
leaving me all bare bones
soaked in someone else's vile
I've become archaic-
A voice lost in someone else's.

Soot rots the roof of my mouth
where you settled your
tasteless language.
The vernacular of antagonists
collapsing my throat from
words I once hoped
would be my own.

The First Time

you ignored my "no",
I have a distinct memory of my stomach churning and
twisting and curling and contouring
into a bow.

Like the kind you rip off your presents during Christmas
except this was not a gift.
I should have known by the shape of your pocket-knife
fingertips that the tool you used so loosely was
not the only sharp object
in the room.

When I shook my head from side to side, your palms
gripped the skin around my lips
like they wanted to mold themselves into a mask.
Halloween was always my favorite holiday,
never yours. But I learned quickly that
monsters roam our world, and I
was giving one a home.

Moisture stained my cheeks as your legs pressed down
onto my thighs like concrete slab.
Cold, heavy,
holding me in place,
like the grip of your threats weren't strong enough to
keep me in my space.
To be honest, for a long time, they were.

I want you to know that
my *I love you*s
were never an invitation
to cover my canvas with your pastels.

Blues and purples healed
into yellows and reds.

I used those words to justify
the bruises beneath
my hipbones that resemble
the pieces of a xylophone.
My waist sang a melody that you
pretended not to know the words to,
your fingertips burned a harmony
that would never match mine.

The second time you ignored my *no*
Your lips shattered against my skin like glass,
and it was raining.
Shrapnel lodged itself into my spine.
My limbs went numb.
I tasted metallic on my tongue.
My ears wouldn't stop ringing, but I know
that my voice didn't shake.

My lips started writing you a letter.
I just kept saying that I was sorry.
I'm sorry for the way that I used my memories
as a sheet for my bed and
I'm sorry for the way that they left
stains on *your* favorite moments.
I said *no* and
The echo of your pillow-fight
palms against the wall
was a reminder of the
force behind your fists.

The third time you ignored my *no*
it turned into the fourth, the fifth, the thirteenth,
I don't know anymore.
It was always those fists that hid the exit signs,
it was the palms around my throat
that made me lose
my voice.

I lost count.
I lost count of the times that you ignored the protests,
the picket signs in my eyes and the
body-mind union strikes.

The last time you ignored my *no*,
I finally realized that I had never been
answering a question.

I kept writing the letter.
I'm sorry for the day that I'll tell you
that you are the worst thing to ever happen to me.
I forgot that honesty
can feel like a noose wrapped around your throat,
searching for a bannister.
I'm sorry that I learned about autonomy.
I closed my lips for the last time.
I didn't know that my voice mattered
I didn't know that my *no*'s had meaning, so
I threw away the letter.

In my lesson on sovereignty
I learned to never raise
a white flag.
To conquer your territory, you only raise red.
Like the lips that rang with objection
My anatomy
cannot be bargained for.

In reality,
I wrote the apology letter for myself
because
I don't owe you a damn thing.

Not my body,
not my sorrys.

Borrowed god

I started writing to your god.
The one you're always talking about.
The one that you say has given you your purpose to live,
the same one that took mine away.

I've been told to start with confessions.
Let my sins bleed from my fingertips,
stain the paper with deviled stories,
ask him to forgive me.

By the time I got to the sixth page, I put
an asterisk, wrote *more to come.*
It seems like try to survive
is sin.

The seventh page started like a new letter.
Maybe he'd forget by then that his sins have
hallowed me into this
letter writer.
Maybe he'll give me
this favor.

Dear Borrowed God,
We haven't spoken before,
I don't think.
I don't know much about you, except that
I don't believe we'd ever get along.
I hope you'll forgive me for that.
I'm writing as a final try.

I've been told that everyone pleads for you
when they're as sick as me.
When they're even sicker than me, the pleading turns
into more of a begging but I promise

that I'm not here to beg.
I'm not looking for a space in your home when
I finally finish rotting,
I'm not asking you to cure me.
I don't take you as a magic maker.
To be honest,
I don't take you for much at all.

I stopped practicing living when
I lost interest in it.
I found myself counting down calendar days.
Crossing off dates in anticipation like
the end would be a holiday, but really
it'd just be an end.
I might be a bit too excited,
I was hoping you could help me with that.

I know that to covet is a task you ask us
not to embark on, but I've been
envying every successful suicide story
wonder if their palms were stretched
towards someone like you.
I like to picture my feature in a newspaper
always hoping for the obituary section,
I once swallowed a pill for every day of the month
that I hated myself,
vomited that up in the enclosed walls of an ambulance.
I don't want to be afraid of death,
I just don't want to reach for it either.

I've learned that you can turn water into wine,
that you can see and hear all that your creations do.
That you are present in all lives but
have you saved anyone, lately?

I heard that you reward good deeds.
That Satan is the punisher of bad ones,
does that put you two on the same level?

You ignore the damaged of your created.
The ones who breathe sin because
that's all they know.
The ones who don't believe in you.

You're someone else's God, and
I'm writing because I was told to.

This wasn't the best choice.

4th of July

It's the fourth of July and I'm thinking of you.
When I was younger, I thought about the
get-togethers. The picnics. Barbecues and
lukewarm beer.
I used to think about the sparklers and how they
made me feel like magic reached out
from my fingertips. It's different now.
I'm always stuck on you.

My mind revels on the red stripe of your pants,
the one you always wore proudly.
I think of a flag
I've never seen you salute.
I always admired that about you.
The way your pride wasn't packed into
false nationality, you just wanted to make your mom proud.

It's the fourth of July and
we're supposed to be celebrating independence, but
the war left so many unable to be alone.
They sacrificed their sanity for these celebrations.
I'm always wondering where the justice in that is.
The way that colorful bombs above our heads make people
clap and cheer but there will always be someone down the block
taking three sleeping pills just to
make it through the fireworks.

It's the fourth of July and
I'm thinking of the stories you told me.
How you still see your platoon exploding,
echoes of the bomb hitting your back with
fists of siege, the numbing in your jaw.
How the bulletproof windows of your Humvee shatter.
You saw fire in your peripheral vision, but couldn't run.

You just missed the hit but
your five closest friends were all gravel and ash,

It's the fourth of July and I'm sorry.

I can still see you.
The way your green eyes turned to the dust of a warzone.
You told me the worst place on earth was inside
a military mind;
all gun-shot residue from m-16 fingertips.
You point them at quick-paced loved ones before
you know what you're doing.
I didn't know the living could haunt you.

It was all bruised ribcages with your
back to the wall. The letter would be found
in the gun powder in your mouth;
there's no need to write answers for questions
that no one will have.
You put the gun to your head.
Practiced a motion you wish you'd never learned,
squeezed the trigger.

Before the bullet infiltrated your skull,
you saw yourself getting married at twenty.
Licked the icing off a cake you made for your mom
the day she beat breast cancer.
Stretched your arms around your little sister the day
you were being deployed.
Watched your wife turn from
stone to sand in
the weight of your PTSD diagnosis.
Felt the bullet hit your brain,
everything went black.

You could feel your military buzz cut
splatter against the white wall behind you.
Blood drip down from your left temple onto your

blue jacket. The last bit of evidence from the trauma
we've caused.
Another mess this country will never claim.

It's the fourth of July and I'm missing you.

The ghost of you left your body,
you never came back to us.
I guess you were gone long before
the metal against
your skin.

Shaky palms and lock-jawed
fingertips.
You set the gun down.
It was empty.

LGBARTWORK

You are all acting like loving all colors
is the crime here,
like the silver touch of a woman and
the teal touch of a man both on my skin
will collide together to make muck but you're really
just afraid of a love that's bigger than yours.

My first "I love you" went to a boy
who dripped his rose-colored cheeks onto
my skin, crafted a masterpiece
out of a broken canvas. His arms blocked
the chill of a blue night
where I thought I needed to pick
one shade.
There was a professor in his
love, the lesson plans taught me
that even the pigments that are hard to
place are worth exploring.

When I moved on
everyone thought my hands
would be stained.
Like I'd never grip a girl's gold
without turning it to rust.
But when I hold a woman in my arms,
I only see the coral carvings of her
confessions, the light pink tint of lips
I want to kiss.
I don't wrap her in my arms
like a gender.
She would never be a place holder
for a grey phase they
thought I was stuck in.

I've been called a “dyke”
by every person who doesn't understand
that my sky dust eyes see every color on equal plains.
I guess it's hard to understand for someone
who had their favorite color picked out for them
in the blanket they were wrapped in
on the day they were born.
So please,
twist your mind around the conversation of a
pale picture I painted the day I told you;
I love the scarlet specks of
a women's skin on mine.

Did it confuse you when I said
the indigo taste of a man's tongue
rested just as easily on my lips?
Or how a person with two colors
instead of one check marked box of a
birth certificate
fit into my palms like artwork?

I'm not a man, but when I see my best friend
look into the eyes of his sapphire lover
I could sing a melody for boys to learn
when strangers see "FAGGOT" written on a banner
wrapped around their mouths.
We'd dance to the rhythm of purple spirits
for every body burned
in the past
by people who thought love
was made for pink and blue.

"Queer" burns the
ears of an older generation.
It was a word used as a whip that left
metallic stains on their teeth.
Maybe it's all the bite marks
paper macheted into my skin,

but it's the only word that can categorize
the way I love.

It was the multicolor touch of a palette
that taught me I could do the same.
I cover my fingertips into the acrylics
of a rainbow.
I smear the dye across my chest like a name tag.
I wear it for the kids who had to
braid their water colors into a rope,
who hung in their closet
like irony.
I wear it for the witches who
were drowned while holding
their lovers hand.

This love was never the crime here.
Ignorance was.

Home Sweet Home

It's the sunray spackles on my pale back, and the red vintage
rug on my living room floor that make me want to buy
one of those cheesy "Home Sweet Home" signs.
The kind that people only ever get as gifts because
If it really felt like home, you
          wouldn't need the sign to prove it.

You'd smell it in the chocolate-chip cookie air and feel it
in the green-thumb breeze flowing through your orchids above
the kitchen sink. This is different.
I want the sign to hang as a plaque
above my head to remind me
          I have a home again.

Some mornings, I'll wake up from the chill
coming through my window,
it takes me a moment to realize that I can stay.
          That I want to.

See, I've always had commitment issues with places.
Always had an itch on the side of my ankle that made me
          want to skip the sidewalks of new cities.

Staying too long always made me feel stagnant.
Which in theory, isn't a good thing to be.
I forget that trees are planted so they could grow.
That without stop signs,
          we'd wake to morning car crashes.

I could blame my aversion to homes by the
twenty-three I had and lost
in my first fourteen years, but it could be
from all the concrete I swallowed every time I
tripped up on denial.
          Having a home always tasted like hard places.

When the last four places you stayed gave you
rug-burn on the welcome mat.

Sometimes living in a space that you don't fit into
feels like being reprimanded for dishonesty.
Like the brick walls know all the secrets you've been keeping
and they want to bury you;
drip pieces of your lies from the drywall,
paint chips splatter onto your artwork and
        expose you.

I've heard people say that someone's home is an extension of
themselves,
I want to know about someone without a home.

Are they so full of who they are that they don't need one?
Are they not anyone at all?
I know that as a kid,
        I considered myself a bad-luck charm

I thought that eviction was etched into a pattern
through the freckles on my face.

I barely remember all the elementary schools
I went to, but I remember hiding an eviction notice from my
mom
in a diary for so long, that when the police came to say
our thirty days were overdue, I told them
that it didn't count if
        she didn't read it.

I can't remember every street we walked and
slept on, but I'm here now.
I've been thinking of finding a local shop
that engraves permanence into wood.
I'll grab a "My First Home" sign,

hang it on the solid wall above my bed.
I'll sing Home Sweet Home
when I see it.

forming addictions with things i never had

i started chain smoking from someone else's smoke cloud.
i thought their grief would make my death
live longer.
i've never actually put a cigarette to my lips, but
i've kissed so many people with black lungs
you'd think i had-
breathing in their lost hope sometime between 2 and 6am
letting the fragrance of a cancerous lust fill my chest.
i'm waiting for the day my hair runs thin and the
skin between my fingers yellow.

there's something refreshing about the pessimism that
soaks the tongues of my weekend lovers, always
reminding me not to make a home out of forlorn fucks.
sometimes, i do it anyway-
it's strange, finding safety
in the arms of someone who's
left lashes against your
chest, letting palms fill with blood
that won't remain in your skin,
how someone's hands that stain someone else's bedsheets
hang like a welcome sign around your throat.

i can't see through to anything when
it's drowned out by someone else's breath.
my mouth runs dry so i
pull the air between my teeth trying to reel in
any hope dangling on the edges of
chapped lips.

my bed weighs heavy with someone else's body
that isn't even there.
a place to bury the nicotine jitters i get each morning
that i'm missing someone gone.

i'm always forming addictions with things i've never had.
the absence made a grave between me and a good night's rest

air burns frigid against my cheek as i taste worries
that never used to navigate my mind
i hold hands with heart ache
dressed as human bodies
let the blood cake around my fingertips
every time my grip is too strong.

Bookmarks in Moments

I see you in the spines of
every book I read,
Your fingerprint hidden
between the lines
I've already read and
always flip back to.
The stories creased into every doggy-tagged page,
an entire novel printed
into the places I never intended
on skipping-
I find myself skimming over dialogue when it feels
too drawn out.
I've always been a little too eager to know the ending.
How it feels.
If every chapter felt unfinished, or if
foreshadowing warns for a plot change
I'm too afraid to face.

I've lost bookmarks in moments and mourned their loss.
Let them dress the page in enough smudge that I can
convince myself that there isn't anything hidden
in what I can't see.

I want to press my eyes shut.
Persuade myself to learn braille;
against your skin,
a sleeve you left out for me.

Maybe I'd read so slowly that I could finally
understand.
Maybe I'd read so slowly that I'd be okay
if I didn't understand.
Maybe touch on risen stories could turn
a hardcover into a soft one,

maybe I'd stop flipping pages
that I never wanted to overturn.

Every word I write is an anagram of your name.
I'm hoping you can hear me calling from
a notebook. Your voice spills from
my pen onto unsuspecting blank pages that
never really felt blank to me.
As if emptiness never wanted to show itself
until it was filled.

I stashed you into every stanza I put to paper and
tried to make sense of.
Is poetry anything, if not admitting
you can't make sense of yourself?

Nothing has felt finished in months.
My own lines looking up at me with
your eyes, knowing things were left
unsaid or unseen.
I know that I've made
an enemy of myself.
I know I let you down.
I'm still hoping my mistakes
aren't as permanent as the letters
I cross out in pen.
Because I've never felt you
there,
in that mess.
I've filled journals
so that I'd never
lose sight of you.
I kept filling in lines with
pencil shavings,
ink stains
that felt like your skin.

I can hear your voice
in everything I read with
my own handwriting.
Whispering everything I refused to hear when I thought
I was listening.
I've been avoiding this.
Just kept hoping each enjambment
in unfinished pieces
would be a catalyst for
fixing things.
I thought I'd forget what having you
looked like
when I included proper punctuation.

As though I could find a way
to erase years of memories
if only your breath
left my papercut palms.
As if your hair would fall
from the
pressed pages of my favorite novel and every
fingerprint you left in my notebook
would fade away.

I swear,
I'd do anything to avoid writing
the
last line of a poem.

Sick

What if
I told you that my body suffocates itself
    when it tries to breath, or that
    my hope is a flooded basement?
What if
    my eyes see sharp objects where
    my hands once were?
Or,
    I stopped believing in anything gentle
        so I traded my hands for knives?
My dreams do not stop when I am
    not sleeping,
my mind is a wasps nest in the way
    it kills itself trying to keep itself alive.

I think, maybe, time climbs
    on top
    of itself.
Everything is happening at once
        but we cannot feel it
        because the rest of the world does and
in humans, empathy is trait
but not a given.

If everything is happening at once but right now
    we live with our feet in the snow,
    hands in our pockets-
        maybe we are building sand-castles, too.
    Maybe we need depression
the same way that a finished puzzle shows
    an entire picture, but you can't ignore
    all the edges
and the way they close the space
            incompletely.

I think I am standing
at the edge of a cliff with
nothing behind me.
I'm sure I provided the terrain
with the glacier
to make the canyon.
I cannot do anything but watch
the way
the water crashes
against the rocks.
I do not know how long until the cliff crumbles-
I'm not sure I'd notice if it already had.

Stories We Share in the Dark

For Cameron

In the glow of a television
we talk about the year past,
my bloody lip,
your sunken eyes in a mirror
you want to crack.

This time
love glides off our mouths
like it's found a residing home,
our whisky skin bathing in the press
of a budding friendship.

We take a deep breath,
our lungs flowered like the storm
didn't touch our pleading hearts.
We're safe now, legs draped
over leather couches where we reach
for the answers from our sharing voices.

The night a reminder
of times we never had,
our bones lit on fire from the good things-
our fervid imaginations
swinging from our words,
a candle-guide
into what "next" looks like.

Suddenly,
the room
bursts into a forest fire
and there has never
been silence.

There's a rush in it

Knowing that someone hates me enough to never let me go,
        using their hands like prison bars
        on my skin.
Make-up fucks pass time while I avoid that edge of longing
for something real,
        or promising,
                or sincere.
Comfort goes a long way.
        It latches at the nape of my neck,
        hiding beneath the mats of my hair just enough
        to feel
        somewhere between
        tranquil and numb.
I've been here before, and I know it.
                My past is elusive.
        I forget lessons I have already learned because
        I'm addicted to hating myself.
I'm destroying myself using
                someone else's hands.
I'm unsure how long it takes to break a habit
                I don't know if I want to.
Loving never sat right in my stomach,
        anxieties twist through my intestines until
        the only thing that cures unease is something
        familiar.
An ache.
Bruises wrapped around my jaw,
        constellations I wish on out of desperation.
Romanticizing the claws snagged into my back is something
        I've always been good at.
        Like there's promise in the inability to let go.
Suffering is where I lay my head at night.
        The rhythmic pattern of a well-acquainted chest.

If I rock back-and-forth in the fetal position long
enough,
I can forget everything that comes after
this.

There is a point that
I need to choose survival.
Rip away the knuckle marks searing my cheekbones.
Unmark the grave that's buried beneath my eyelids,
Forgive myself for letting it get this far.

I am more than whatever I've been telling myself.
Compassion spills from survivor's lips even after
being sealed.
There is a dishonesty ripping the skin around the mouth
that let me think of myself as less-than.
I am enough. I am
enough.
I am enough.
I am not composed of other people's words.

There's a rush in it
knowing that someone cares enough to never
hold on too tightly,
using their hands like welcome mats
on my skin.
I'm growing familiar with a touch
that has only ever been gentle.
When my name isn't laced in scolding,
it doesn't tear at the wounds the way it used to.
It dances at the edge of my hairline,
reveals the stories I'm not afraid to share.

I'm becoming well acquainted with
the echoes of the laughter
I thought I had lost.
Loving isn't so foreign, anymore.

Skyler Jaye Rutkowski is a poet from Buffalo, NY. She represented her city in the 2017 National Poetry Slam, volunteers at Just Buffalo Literary Center, and runs the monthly open mic series Poetry at Perks. Her work has appeared or is forthcoming in: Emrys Journal, Rhythm & Bones YANYR Anthology, My Next Heart: New Buffalo Poetry, and more. You can generally find her at a local coffee shop nose-deep in a book, planning her latest travel itinerary, or anywhere she can pet a doggo. Find her tweeting her existential crisis @SkylerJaye23

33553352R00026

Made in the USA
Middletown, DE
18 January 2019